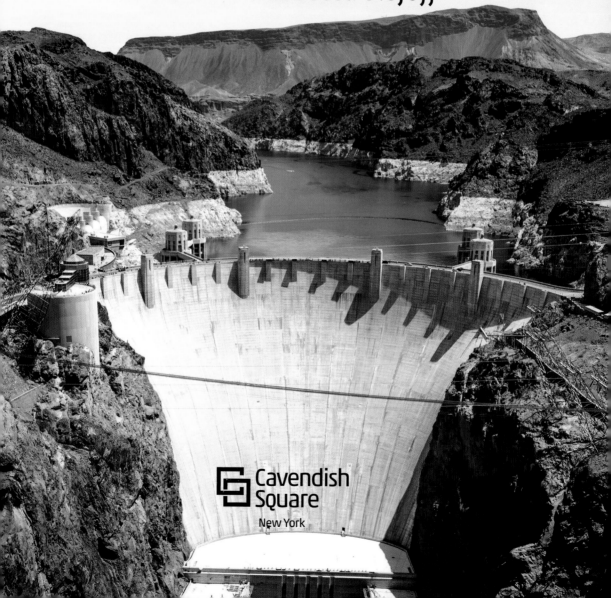

Engineering
North America's
Landmarks

Building the Hoover Dam

Rebecca Stefoff

Cavendish
Square

New York

Published in 2018 by Cavendish Square Publishing, LLC
243 5th Avenue, Suite 136, New York, NY 10016

Copyright © 2018 by Cavendish Square Publishing, LLC

First Edition

Website: cavendishsq.com

This publication represents the opinions and views of the author based on his or her personal experience, knowledge, and
research. The information in this book serves as a general guide only. The author and publisher have used their best efforts
in preparing this book and disclaim liability rising directly or indirectly from the use and application of this book.

All websites were available and accurate when this book was sent to press.

Library of Congress Cataloging-in-Publication Data

Names: Stefoff, Rebecca, 1951- author.
Title: Building the Hoover Dam / Rebecca Stefoff.
Description: New York : Cavendish Square Publishing, 2018. | Series: Engineering North
America's landmarks | Includes bibliographical references and index.
Identifiers: LCCN 2017017497 (print) | LCCN 2017022928 (ebook) | ISBN 9781502629715 (E-book) | ISBN
9781502629685 (pbk.) | ISBN 9781502629708 (library bound) | ISBN 9781502629692 (6 pack)
Subjects: LCSH: Hoover Dam (Ariz. and Nev.)--History--Juvenile literature.
Classification: LCC TC557.5.H6 (ebook) | LCC TC557.5.H6 S73 2018 (print) | DDC 627/.820979313--dc23
LC record available at https://lccn.loc.gov/2017017497

Editorial Director: David McNamara
Editor: Fletcher Doyle
Copy Editor: Rebecca Rohan
Associate Art Director: Amy Greenan
Designer: Alan Sliwinski
Production Coordinator: Karol Szymczuk
Photo Research: J8 Media

Printed in the United States of America

Contents

Visitors peer into the Black Canyon from the Hoover Dam visitor center. A bridge crosses the canyon in the background.

The Black Canyon

Settlers from the United States started coming to the Southwest in the 1860s. Native Americans and people from Mexico already lived there. At first, these settlers came to look for gold and other minerals. Then, they came to farm.

The farmers had a problem. The Southwest is a dry area. People needed a water source they could count on.

Southern Nevada, like much of the rest of the American Southwest, has a dry, desert landscape.

By 1900, the growing towns of the Southwest also needed electricity. The answer to both problems was to build a **dam** on the Colorado River. It would be built in Black Canyon. The canyon is 30 miles (48 kilometers) from Las Vegas, Nevada.

Three Reasons to Build a Dam

A dam across the Colorado River would do three things for the people of the Southwest:

1. Water would build up behind the dam. It would form a **reservoir.** It would store water for drinking and farming.

2. Water power at the dam would make electricity.

3. A dam would have **spillways** to help prevent floods.

The Dam Becomes Law

Rivers and streams from seven states flow into the Colorado River. Need for water was growing in the

This is how the Black Canyon of the Colorado River looked before the Hoover Dam was built.

West. The states needed a plan to share the water. Six states signed a plan in 1922. The seventh state, Arizona, signed in 1944.

There was another problem. Congress had to pay for the dam. People outside the Southwest did not want to spend money on it.

Then the Mississippi River flooded in 1927. The floods caused great damage. Congress agreed to pay for new projects to prevent floods. One of them was the Colorado River dam. In 1928, President Calvin Coolidge signed the bill to build the dam.

Flooding along the Mississippi River in 1927 convinced the US Congress to pay for the Hoover Dam.

Hoover Dam By the Numbers

Construction time: April 20, 1931 to March 1, 1936

Dynamite used: 8.5 million pounds (3.9 million kg).

Number of workers: 21,000

Deaths during building: Officially, 96

Cost: $94 million, plus $71 million to build the power plant

Height: 726 feet (221 meters)

Thickness: 660 feet (201 m) at base, 45 feet (13.7 m) at top

Weight: More than 6,600,000 tons (6 million metric tons)

Number of electric generators: 17

Visitors each year: Almost 1 million

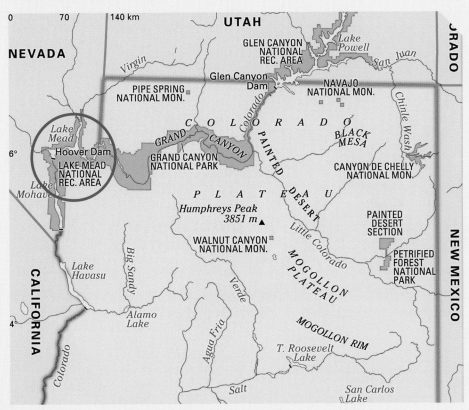

The Colorado River flows from Utah and through the Grand Canyon before it reaches the Hoover Dam (*circled at left*).

Men who worked on the canyon's walls were called "high scalers."

Chapter Two

A Dangerous Job

Building a dam in Black Canyon was a big job. It would take skill. It would take a lot of hard work under the desert sun.

Engineers Make a Plan

Engineers made a plan for building the dam. Engineers solve problems using science and math. A **civil engineer** builds public projects.

Civil engineers designed Hoover Dam in the shape of an arch. It looks like a C. Its curve faces upstream. The dam was made of **concrete** and steel. The shape and materials make the dam very strong.

The river's **current** pushes against the back of the dam. This presses the ends of the dam against

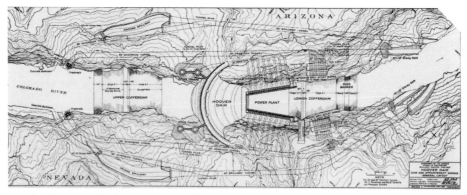

The final plan called for a C-shaped dam to be built across the canyon.

the canyon walls. The arch breaks up the force of the water. It sends the force toward the rock walls.

Hard Times

Hoover Dam was built during the Great Depression. This was a hard time in America. Banks and businesses closed. People lost jobs. Many lost their homes. Some were willing to move anywhere for work.

News spread that a dam would be built in the Black Canyon. There would be work. Thousands of men rushed to the desert. Many brought their families. They formed large camps near Black Canyon. Then Boulder City was built for workers. At one point, more than 5,200 men were working on the dam.

Moving the River

Cables were used to move cement and equipment into place.

Before work could start in Black Canyon, the river had to be moved. This was done with **diversion tunnels.** Four tunnels were needed to move the Colorado River. Two were dug into rock on each side of Black Canyon. The tunnels were 56 feet (17 m) wide. The tunnels added were more than 3 miles (4.8 km) long.

Making tunnels was hard and dangerous. The tunnels were hot, with bad air. Many men became sick. Workers blasted the rock with dynamite. They dug into it with drills. The tunnels carried the river around the dam site. This let people work on the dry river bottom. When the dam was done, parts of the diversion tunnels were closed.

Instead of a single wall, the dam was built up by stacking many forms and pouring concrete into them to make small blocks.

A Dam of Many Parts

Concrete gives off heat when it dries. It takes time for it to cool. It needs to cool to harden. A single wall the size of the Hoover Dam would take more than 125 years to cool.

Hoover Dam was made up of many small blocks of concrete. Steel pipes carried cold water to cool the concrete. When a layer of blocks had cooled, the next layer could be put on top of it.

The concrete used to build Hoover Dam could pave a highway 16 feet (4.9 m) wide across the United States. A total of 582 miles (936.6 km) of steel pipe was needed to cool the concrete.

Shovelers stand ready as wet concrete pours from a huge bucket that hangs from cables. The cables stretch across the top of the canyon.

"Hurry-Up Crowe"

Frank Crowe studied civil engineering. He wanted to build "the biggest dam ever built by anyone anywhere." He got the job building Hoover Dam. He was in charge of all parts of the job.

He had tracks built on the canyon walls. Giant cranes moved along these tracks. Cables attached to the cranes stretched in a web across the canyon. The cranes could move the cables to any point. The cables carried wet concrete in steel buckets. At the busiest time, a 20-ton (18.1 metric ton) bucket of concrete was dumped on the dam every seventy-eight seconds.

Crowe got things done quickly. His nickname was "Hurry-Up Crowe."

Hoover Dam, with its power plant and the mouths of the diversion tunnels below it

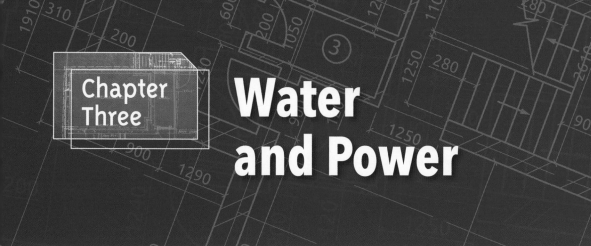

Chapter Three

Water and Power

On September 30, 1935, about ten thousand people gathered to see President Franklin D. Roosevelt declare the Hoover Dam open. "Hurry-Up Crowe" and his workers had finished the dam two years ahead of schedule. Finishing the power plant took a little longer.

Lake Mead

Once the dam was finished, the diversion tunnels were closed near the top. The lower parts are still in use.

With the tunnels blocked, water started to pool behind the dam. This was the beginning of Lake Mead. It is the biggest reservoir in the United States. It provides water for drinking and farming across the Southwest. Lake Mead is also used for outdoor sports. Many people use it for boating.

Lake Mead has not been full since 1983. The lake has shrunk for two reasons. One is a long **drought**. The other reason is that more people now are using the lake's water. In early 2017, the lake's level was 141 feet (43 m) below where it was in 1983.

The lower parts of the diversion tunnels are still important. Two of them are spillways. These are channels that move water around the dam when the water behind it is too high. The other two carry water into the dam's power plant.

When Lake Mead was full in 1983, water gushed into its spillways to keep the dam from overflowing.

Energy from Water

Energy made from flowing or falling water is called **hydroelectricity.**

A hydroelectric dam channels some of the water from its reservoir into a power plant. The water flows quickly down steep pipes. At the bottom of the pipes, the water turns spinning blades. They are fastened to poles that turn. Each pole holds up a generator, which is a machine full of magnets. As the generators turn on the poles, the magnets create electricity.

Massive generators are lined up inside the dam. They produce hydroelectricity. It comes from the energy from flowing or falling water.

Hoover Dam's power plant provides electricity to about eight million people. They live in Arizona, Nevada, and Southern California.

Hoover Dam Today

Hoover Dam was a huge success for American engineering. Still, nearly one hundred people died during the building of the dam. False rumors said that some workers were swallowed up by the concrete poured on the dam. Most deaths were actually from heat or accidents.

For years, Highway 93 ran across the top of the dam. The road into the canyon and back up again had many twists and turns. For easier driving, a new bridge was opened in 2010. It goes across the Black Canyon close to the dam.

People who want to visit the dam still drive down into the canyon. Driving across the top of the dam is no longer allowed.

Today, nearly a million people visit the dam each year. This marvel of engineering still has the power to impress everyone who sees it.

"They died to make the desert bloom" says this memorial to the workers who died while building the dam.

Five Tallest Dams in the United States

1. Oroville Dam: Embankment dam on the Feather River in California stands 770.5 feet (235 m).

2. Hoover Dam: Arch-gravity dam on the Colorado River stands 726 feet (221 m).

3. Dworshak Dam: This dam on the North Fork Clearwater River in Idaho stands 717 feet (219 m).

4. Glen Canyon Dam: A newer concrete arch dam on the Colorado River stands 710 feet (216 m).

5. New Bullards Bar Dam: A concrete arch dam on the North Yuba River in California stands 645 feet (197 m).

Hoover Dam Quiz

1. What did people in the Southwest need before the Hoover Dam was built?

2. How many of the United States share the water of the Colorado River?

3. How did the dam builders move the river water out of the way so they could work?

📍 Glossary

dam A barrier that keeps water from flowing freely.

diversion tunnel A tunnel made to carry river water around the place where the dam is being built.

civil engineer An engineer who makes structures for the public. They make roads, bridges, and dams.

concrete A blend of sand, gravel, cement, and water that is hard and strong when it dries.

current The flow or the speed at which water moves.

drought A long period of no rain.

engineer A person who uses science and math to build things.

hydroelectricity Electric energy made from the force of falling or flowing water.

reservoir The pool or lake that forms behind a dam and stores water; a human-made lake.

spillway An opening or channel for water to flow over, around, or through a dam.

⚲ Find Out More

Books

Halls, Kelly Milner. *The Story of the Hoover Dam*. North Mankato, MN: Cherry Lake Publishing, 2014.

Miller, Heather. *The Hoover Dam*. Chicago: Norwood House Press, 2013.

Websites

Boulder City/Hoover Dam Museum

http://www.bcmha.org

The museum tells the story of the people who built the Hoover Dam.

Building Big: Hoover Dam

http://www.pbs.org/wgbh/buildingbig/wonder/structure/hoover.html

This PBS site details the building of Hoover Dam.

📍 Index

Page numbers in **boldface** are illustrations. Entries in **boldface** are glossary terms.

♀ About the Author

Rebecca Stefoff has written books for young readers on many topics in science, technology, and history. She is the author of the six-volume series Is It Science? (Cavendish Square, 2014) and the four-volume series Animal Behavior Revealed (Cavendish Square, 2014). She also wrote *The Telephone, The Camera, Submarines, The Microscope and Telescope,* and *Robots* for the Cavendish Square Great Inventions series. Stefoff lives in Portland, Oregon.